what we ache for

4/27/11

For Christy & Ralph,

It was so wonderful to meet you!
And, it was a joy to read for you;
Enjoy the book & be well always!

what we ache for
Looking forward to the next

ache for
time I see you.

All best.

———

poetry & prose
by
eric morago

Moon Tide Press

October 2010

What We Ache For
Copyright 2010 by Eric Morago

Editors
Ricki Mandeville
Michael Miller

Graphic design
Michael Wada

Front cover photo
Michael Miller

Back cover photo
Katie O'Shaughnessy

Moon Tide logo design
Ricki Mandeville

What We Ache For
is published by
Moon Tide Press
Anaheim, California
www.moontidepress.com

FIRST EDITION

Printed in the United States of America

ISBN # 978-1-4507-3233-8

CONTENTS

FOREWORD

I think Eric Morago is dreamy.

Really, this isn't about aesthetics, although I've known many a heart to flutter when Eric's boyishly good looks and ink-splattered form spill into the room. This is about the quality of his writing, poems written inches above the ground, what it sounds like in that place between Slumberland and Real Talk. Give him a few minutes of your time coupled with a lease on your ears and heart. He will reward you with fire-breathing and time machines. You will negotiate the sobriety of Norse gods. Or maybe you'll just revisit some old dinosaurs. Whatever field trip Morago takes you on, it always leads back to the poet's front porch, where he's probably sipping a whiskey (no straws please) and looking at the stars, getting misty over the vastness of metaphor and the immediacy of beautiful women. And this is why we are friends.

Every poet at some point delves into an ocean of confessional journalism. What I dig about Eric's work is his Raymond Carver-esque attention to detail. The cinnamon gum. The way the towels smelled. How to properly launch a roll of toilet paper. The minutiae are kept close to his clunky, squishy heart machine. He then takes the self-same machine and manufactures explosions all over the parking lot. He burns and rips carousel music and remixes it into slow dance. He's a multi-tasking son-of-a-pistol, working your head and gut like a boxer in a fifties film. And the thing is, our boy is so smooth with the damage, you'll finish reading this book and wonder where you got those Turin Shroud-shaped bruises. But in the interim, you'll have had tea with your monsters. You'll have relearned the mechanics of bicycles and love. You'll realize that Eric Morago is the air traffic controller on our emotional runway, guiding us towards the place in our hearts that we've closed off for far too long. By the time you've pedaled through the last poem in this book, you'll have learned all the nuances of what we ache for. You may end up thinking, when all is said and done, that he's pretty dreamy as well.

—*Rob Sturma*
Author, Miles of Hallelujah

Let all the misery fall out of your chest.
                    —*Julie Orringer*

We are amazed how hurt we are.
We would give anything for what we have.
                    —*Tony Hoagland*

I

RACING FORWARD

You have never ridden a bicycle,
never had the guts to try.

It is easier when you're younger.
Shaky attempts and falls
don't matter once you get the hang of it,
learn the trick of balance, start zipping
down the block, back and forth,
back and forth, until long after dark
and legs ache from too much freedom.

Any skinned knees from kissing asphalt
at that boyhood age are carried with pride.
More holy than press-on tattoos, scrapes
hardened into scabs prove you're tough—
that you've gone through something.
Your flesh changed because of it.

Scarless at twenty-four, you think
it's how foolish you'd look your first time,
which has kept you from trying. How virgin
muscles uncertain of their movement
would cause you to crash, again and again.

Still, though, propelled by the body kinetic,
racing forward is something to desire.
That glorious moment you start to rush
away from safe things towards a world
that can hurt you, and you're ready
for it. You're hungry for it.

That is the heart of this fear—
that once you learn how,
you will ride off so fast,
so fast you will forget

what safe ever was.

THINGS I'D TELL MY 13-YEAR-OLD SELF
(HAD I A TIME MACHINE)

When mom says, *it's time to throw out your old comic books*,
don't listen. Hide them under the mattress; she'll assume
you're hoarding *Playboys* and not ask questions.

Take Spanish freshman year, so when your friends plot against
you, using words you've never heard before, you won't get caught
with your *pantalones* down in front of the whole junior varsity
cheer squad.

Switch from tighty-whiteys to boxers.

The summer your grandmother moves in, don't spend so much time
at the arcade. Stay home on the couch with her in the afternoons
watching the O.J. Simpson trial. Memorize what a room feels like
with her in it.

Despite that one episode of *Saved By the Bell*, beer is not evil.

Fight the temptation to take a road trip to Boise after you graduate.
Eighteen hours is too long a drive to find out she doesn't like you
that way.

Under no circumstances are you to sketch the girls you have crushes
on and send the drawings to them in the mail. Do, however, write
poems about them—terrible, awful poetry—shoeboxes full of folded,
crumpled notebook paper that you can one day use for kindling when
you're old enough to start a really good blaze.

SMEAR

I maimed and killed so many butterflies in my youth.
Sure, like other boys my age, I doused whole armies
of ants with hose water, squished spiders and crickets,
examining their gooey remains, but I took delight
in butterflies. As they'd flutter from one flower bud
to the next, I would pinch their wings between index
and thumb and witness their legs scuffle furiously,
their tiny heads twist side to side, and their abdomens
writhe forward and back, until there was no more fight
in them. They would just stare up in a calm moment
before I'd rip them apart. Sometimes I only yanked
an antenna or leg. Other times, their proboscis, robbing
them of a means to taste, or I'd tear off their wings,
grounding them, reminding them what it is to crawl,
just to watch as they would madly try to make sense
of the earth their legs were now held captive to, while
their luckier brethren soared above them unnoticing.
Then with wings still pressed between my fingertips,
I remember rubbing back and forth, wearing them
down into a chalky dust that vanished in the breeze,
like ash, until nothing remained—but a faint smear
on my skin, left behind from their phantom shine.

SPACKLE

1.

Swelling with adolescent piss
and vinegar, I ruptured like acne,
exploded and hurled a coffee mug
at my mother. I cannot recall why,

other than for the mad schools
of chemical fish under my skin
all frenzy and chaos—impulses
I did not understand, nor knew

how to control. My aim was off,
but the way she cried boulders
when it shattered against the wall,
I knew, even missing, I still hit her.

2.

It takes minutes to repair a hole
in a wall, much longer to accept
how it got there. Shoveling spackle
with two fingers, I smeared it over

the gorge. Then, with a knife,
I scraped the paste down smooth,
until everything was again perfect.
My mother looked on and said,

one day we'll forget. Unsure who
these words were meant to comfort
more, I did not believe them; knew
I'd carry the memory like a tumor,

a lump of tactile regret pushing
against my brain. But for her,
I hoped she was right, that she'd
remember nothing of that day.

3.

My mother remembers little
of anything these days. Her
neurons are confused kamikaze
butterflies, killing themselves

in flashes of fluttering madness,
head swelling from a disease
I call "Monster." The times
I was more a short fuse stick

of dynamite than a son are just
scenes from a film she thinks
she saw once. *Never her boy,*
she tells me. *Never her boy.*

I'd give back every violent
moment—fill each hole with
tales of an exploding child, if
it meant she'd just remember

my name. But all I can do
is speak fog in a gusty room
where words fail, and a fierce
rage returns to my body again.

REPERCUSSIONS

No more poems about the moon.
                              —Michael Roberts

Upon hearing this, the moon left—
walked out for a pack of smokes,
after she promised to return in five
minutes. The next morning we found
slivers of her disappointment scattered
everywhere—toothbrushes snapped,
the halves tossed in our toilets, stiletto
heels smashed through the computer
screens of all poets, and snow globes
forced down the throats of garbage
disposals worldwide. When glass
shards crunched in the metal teeth
of sink drains, we knew she wasn't
coming back, that we took her lunar
sensitivity for granted. We forgot
how she obsessed over her shifting
gut—how some nights she was ghost
thin and others so full, our own bellies
swelled from her glow. She hung on
each metaphor, all the times we swore
she lived in our lovers' eyes made her
feel so, so beautiful. Now she's gone.
In time, a strange species, light-years
away, if they are lucky may come to
know her, write poetry in alien speak,
or perhaps woo her telepathically with
thoughts so flattering she forgets our
planet's harsh name from her tongue.
She will call that rock home and we
will be on this one struggling to see
the beauty in streetlamps and traffic
lights—enough to compare love to,
but will find ourselves lacking.

ENTANGLED

A beautiful portrait of destruction,
her back is tattooed from shoulder
to shoulder—a giant octopus tears
boats apart with unworldly tendrils.
This turns me on. I am a prepubescent
again thinking I've found ambrosia
between the pages of Victoria's Secret
catalogues. I get dizzy, lost in fantasy.
How though its body is submerged
in murky water, hidden by shading,
I believe the monster is winking at me.
I sit, imagine freckles into tiny frenzied
sailors jumping ship into the dark of her
skin, sinking down spine's curve,
drowning, or falling into the creature's
waiting, open-beaked mouth. I would
never tell her any of this, of course.
Better she stay in the deep, a shadowy
figure of myth. And like a yarn-spinning
seadog swearing by fantastical beasts—
all tentacles, sharp snouted and snarl
toothed—I too am ensnared, imagination
entangled in the suction-cupped arms
of wanting. It is all I can do to fight,
struggle being pulled under an inky
veil where our eyes can clearly meet,
where any and all mystique is gone.

I HOPE SHE FINDS CALLING ME BACK
JUST AS DIFFICULT

I hate asking girls out over the phone.
Would-be conversations have a way
of turning into beasts of uncertainty
eviscerating courage, dangling
bloodied doubt before me.

I get through five digits
before I am swallowed whole
by that merciless wretch
and left forever dateless
in the pit of its stomach.

I hang up the phone.
Try again.
Dupe myself into thinking
that rejection wouldn't mash my ego
into a runny glob of nerves
lacking anything solid
like a backbone.

Her machine picks up.
The beast ensnarls my diction
and I choke out incoherent words
asking her to call me back.

Waiting
I am sluggishly digested
in uncertainty's lonely gut.

HOW TO SAY I LOVE YOU, FOR THE FIRST TIME

1. Learn origami. Practice folding paper into strange creatures.
2. Keep your fingers loose to avoid cramping.
3. Commit the precision of the art to memory, so you can do it blindfolded. When the time comes, you may find yourself in pitch dark.
4. Study calligraphy.
5. Spend at least an hour each night writing *love* with every letter of the alphabet until you've spelled out words like *orange*, *xylophone* or *menagerie*, and they all remind you of her.
6. When you are ready, remove your heart, gently.
7. Spell *love* across it using only the letters of her name.
8. Fold the heart into any animal she desires.
9. Place it in her hand.
10. Don't expect anything in return.

BREAKING UP IS HARD TO DO, SO MAY I SUGGEST YOU

Start a game of hide and seek. Don't seek.

Stage your own kidnapping. For the sake of believability, send
a severed thumb or ear in the mail. Using your own thumb or ear
is, of course, optional.

Find Jesus. If you've already found Him, find L. Ron Hubbard.

Build a robot 'you' and have it marry her. Everybody wins.
Note: Don't exaggerate any anatomical features of said robot,
as she may be the wiser.

Play dead. It works for possums.

Join a traveling circus. This may, however, require of you talents
such as juggling, tight rope walking or lion taming. If you lack these
skills, join a monastery. This may, however, require abstaining from
drinking, sex and talking. If this is not for you, join a book club—
in the Arctic.

Buy a roll of gauze, wrap it around your forehead, and fake amnesia.

Draw suspicion that you are a serial killer. Save news clippings of
unsolved murders and make a scrapbook. Scotch tape locks of hair
and fingernails to its pages, leaving it open and conspicuously
placed. *Note:* Do not attempt this if you are now, or have ever been,
a serial killer.

Tattoo another girl's name across your chest. If this fails, tattoo a man's.

Write *this* poem. Slip it in the empty wine bottle you kept from your
first night together, back when your heart swelled and everything was
forever and ever. Place it on her doorstep; ring the bell and then walk
away, never looking back, even when you hear the glass shatter.

DELIQUENCY

My cheek is the curse word you love rolling
your tongue over. My earlobes, the pennies

you always *take* from the tray, but never *leave*.
My mouth, a pool you swim in, without waiting

thirty minutes after eating. My neck, the prank
call you make when bored, all creepiness and

heavy breath. My spine, the last page you skip
ahead to read, before starting the first chapter.

My ribs, every mattress tag you've ever removed.
My penis is your favorite street to jaywalk across.

My confidence is a doorbell you ditch. My heart,
the lonely game of solitaire you feel compelled

to cheat at. And my head is a crowded room
where you will forever cry wolf.

POEM FOR THE EX, WHO HATED POETRY

Your attention span
sucks, so I wrote this haiku.
I know you cheated.

OPEN HEART SURGERY

Cut me open, she says,
bringing his stethoscope hands
up to her chest. Listening

with his fingers, he expects
to feel thunder, but can only
make out a murmur.

This concerns him.
He takes out his scalpel.
Her skin is lace peeled back

revealing the anatomy
of every past relationship.
He is surprised how easy it is

to undress her. Lying there
under his examination, she
points to her heart and says,

These scars, I tell myself,
are learned. Make me forget.
She begs him. He inspects

the muscle, the abundance
of scar tissue surrounding it,
then satisfied, closes the incision.

Why didn't you fix it? she asks.
He wishes he could convince her
that it's no accident the heart

resembles a clenched fist,
built to take and give a beating.
But he doesn't. He can tell

she's not much of a fighter.
Instead he refers her to a
plastic surgeon and says,

When he's through, even you
won't be able to recognize it.

COSMO OFFERS HOW TO FIND MR. RIGHT

She considers reading the article, wants to dissect
its instruction like a frog's belly, cut into the meat
and learn the biology of it all, but doesn't.

Instead she sinks lower into couch cushions,
mixed drink in hand, some spiced rum concoction
that tastes like vacation. It's been a long day.

The cable box's LED glows seven, reminds her
she is running late for dinner with the new boy.
He, a beautiful average, has a smile of red licorice

and a good vocabulary—uses words she doesn't
recognize in compliments she's not heard before.
If this prince were a frog, he'd be basking behind

terrarium glass in some pet store. She wishes
she could keep one more exotic, speckled wild
with color, so dangerous a creature it sweats

a poison used to coat the tips of arrowheads.
This boy perspires saccharine, his brow beads
gum drops. She is certain if she were to travel

his chest with her tongue, move lower, there'd
be no bite of salt to speak of. But he's magazine
subscription dependable and *that has to count*

for something has become her new mantra.
However, tonight she cannot repeat the chant
enough to want to like him. He finally phones,

asking where she is. *Sorry*, she offers softly.
A friend is going through a really hard time.
I need to be there for her tonight. She hopes

her lie is so obvious he never thinks to call
again. He hangs up. She mourns the dead
line as much she would a stranger's corpse

at a funeral. She knows she should feel bad,
but doesn't. Finishing her rum, she puts down
the empty glass, picks up *Cosmo* and reads.

AFTER THIS MORNING

I am brushing my teeth with her toothpaste.
A tang of mint stronger than I prefer,
but it's there on that sink top, convenient,
like bodies are after too much to drink,

like excuses for actions, and like beds.
We are sharing the space of her hotel
room's vanity sink and she is wrapped in
one of their terry cloth towels, whiter

than white and smelling of far too much bleach.
We are close enough to smell such things, but
keep enough polite distance between us
to remind ourselves we are still strangers

here. And we will be after this morning,
after these limbs of flesh have shaken
the memory of the other like fall leaves.
But right now, on the ridge of her shoulder

beads of water rest in that uncertain
moment, before they grow too heavy, lose
their perfection and glide down skin. I am
pretending not to notice this, afraid

if she catches me she will think I want
to know too much—the name of the first boy
to break her heart, or everything she hates
about herself. Instead I lean over,

swish and spit the minty froth from my mouth,
and watch it spiral under the running
faucet just before it disappears, washed
away like a name, and someday a face.

WHAT MY MONSTER WANTS

Its wailing, a fury of jackhammers
clogging its throat like chunks of bone
in a garbage disposal, keeps me awake.

What the hell is wrong with you, monster?

Nothing, it sobs.

I do my best to ignore the beast, fixate
on stucco overhead as if stargazing,
wishing it would just tire itself out already.

But it does not relent, whines like a dog
behind a closed door, like a child
lost in a department store.

Annoyance turns to concern. I lean
over my bed, peer into the darkness
beneath and ask again.

Please, tell me, why are you crying?

Because you are not afraid anymore.

The creature is right.

Though its face is still the gargoyle's
nightmare I remember, what was once
fear to look upon it, has turned to pity.

I'm still afraid. Just not of you, I say,
confessing fears as if they were sins
for which I sought absolution.

Airplanes.
Going to the dentist.
Geese.
Opening my driver's-side door on a busy street.

My credit score.
The Mayan calendar.
Knuckles cracking.
Red wine when wearing a new shirt.
Children with sticky fingers.
Finding cancer before I find love.
Dying and being wrong about God...

Wow, it interrupts.

What?

How do you EVER sleep at night?
my monster asks, grinning,
before turning on its side,
and finally dozing off—

for a second, I believe I can too.

But those fears I've let out stay
circling above me now—starved
vultures over wounded prey.

Certain they will tear into flesh
as soon as I close my eyes,
I surrender to a restless night.

Staring at the ceiling, measuring
the wingspan of each of my fears,
waiting for morning to come.

WWJD

At a blackjack table in Vegas
a clean-cut twenty-something-year-old
without a stain of the city's sin on him
sits to my left showing a five and a six.

When his bet comes around
he is puzzled as to how to play the game
like he's five again learning to go fish.

Around his right wrist
he wears a *What would Jesus do?* bracelet.

Jesus would double down.

LETTERS TO GIRLS, NEVER SENT

Dear, I cannot recall your name, but when you took
my hand, raised it to your four-year-old grin like a cookie
and bit down hard—those tiny teeth marks pressed into
the chubby flesh of my palm; I thought they'd never fade

and at only four and a half, believed it was love. *Katie M,*
back in fifth grade you broke your arm and I sat with you
a full week of recess drawing dinosaurs on your cast—
remember? That summer you moved to Idaho.

Before you left, I wanted to tell you how you made
my eleven-year-old heart kick. Instead I teased you
about potatoes. *To Samantha my first kiss,* you were
all country and cinnamon gum the first time our tongues

slow danced in the gymnasium of our teenage mouths,
Garth Brooks playing, crooning about fire and women.
For six months I found myself listening to country songs
and chewing Big Red. I'd like you to know I no longer listen

to that crap, but I still buy a pack of your favorite gum
when I want to remember fifteen. *Dear Born Again
who didn't act like it,* you could make a boy dizzy
every time you took off your top, and confused

every time you'd put it back on, crying. *To Katie M
(again),* my last night in Idaho we found a cornfield maze;
spent the evening getting lost. The next morning, I tried
to write this letter but couldn't. Rather, by your bed I left

a potato. I haven't heard from you since. *To the girl
I lost my virginity to (whose name I cannot repeat
because her now-husband is much larger than I,
has anger issues and a gun collection),* thank you.

It was awesome. *To the girls in all the bars*, I'm sorry.
I know none of you were interested in me, but when
I drink that much, I think everyone is interested in me.
Katie W, you had eyes like violins and a smile like gravity.

I fell. You didn't. *Sascha,* your reckless driving reminded
me how when the right two people meet, they crash.
To the ex, Krystal, your name, implied you were delicate.
You were not. I was the one to shatter, to break.

In your own way, you made me a poet, taught me
the company of good metaphor, how the chest
is full of them, how when we hurt they rally and rise
up the spine to the brain to speak lightning, so hope

sparks behind tear ducts when we need it. When you left,
I cried a lot of lightning. *Dear future falling partner,*
you will know me by my mailbag full of letters to girls,
never sent. Together we will take it, scatter the contents

above our heads—a ritual I usually practice alone—
and watch the letters stick in the air like constellations.
Sitting under them, you may ask, *Why are there so many?*
And I'll say, *Because the nights were so dark,*

I needed them all up there, to find my way to you.
You will call me three types of cheese, before I feel
a pang in my left hand and find an impression of teeth
you tell me this time will not fade.

II

LIPS

"Have you ever had a lap dance?" the *girl* asked, pulling me up out of the audience.

"No," I confessed.

Mandy and the rest of her friends seated at our table erupted in laughter—the kind foreboding humiliation. Something wasn't right. I had just excused myself from our table to go to the restroom, and upon my return it was obvious I had missed some joke. As the show's hostess hurried me up to the stage, I could tell I was in trouble—it was as clear to the eye as the bulge in her crotch.

***

When I fall for a girl, my common sense doesn't just take off on a quick weekend getaway. It goes on sabbatical and sends postcards. Dignity be damned, I will make a fool of myself for a girl that makes my heart kick. Mandy was no exception. I met her on New Year's Eve at a friend's party when she tied me to the stairwell banister with a tropical lei and proceeded to make out with me. I have no idea where said lei came from; when a beautiful woman ties one to anything with a lei, one must simply accept it without question. Later, after she untied me, I learned that Mandy was a nursing student from San Diego, and was spending her winter break in Long Beach visiting a friend who she saw very little of during the busy semester. Since she was going to be local for the next few weeks, we tried dating.

Things went well enough at first. We had a similar sense of humor, there was a definite physical chemistry between us, we both liked sushi, and on our first date we discovered a shared love for skee-ball. We spent over two hours at a Dave and Buster's trying doggedly to beat the other's high score as if we were playing for the prize title of international champion. In between bouts of smack-talking and boasting, we delved into X-rated conversation.

"Where's the craziest place you've had sex?" she asked, flashing me a grin so hot it could melt an ice age.

"An elevator," I lied. I'd never had sex outside of a bedroom.

"What about you?" I asked, hoping she couldn't beat my bluff.

"Outside my house on the front porch with my parents home."

"Oh."

Damn.

However, despite the promise of things heating up between us, it ended abruptly in a Starbucks. After a week, she'd decided that the timing was bad.

"I'm sorry," she said. "But, I just don't think I'm emotionally available to be doing this right now."

"And, what *are* we doing right now?" I asked, confused. To the best of my knowledge, dating for a week wasn't supposed to be a huge stress.

I tried convincing her to just let things play out and that I didn't need her to be emotionally available for me. A week was way too soon to be worrying about those sorts of things, and I wasn't looking for a relationship.

"I know. I'm sorry. I really, really like you, but I don't want to explore these feelings. I'm not in a good place. I just want to be friends. Is that okay?" She *it's-not-you-it's-me'd* me like a champ. But I couldn't be upset with her; I have a soft spot for emotionally indecisive women.

"Of course. I won't say that I'm hurt. But I am bummed. I was—*I thought we were*—having a lot of fun. If things ever change, and I'm not seeing anyone, hit me up. You know…if things do change."

She agreed, "If things change."

A few phone calls, a lunch and three weeks later, she was back in San Diego. School started up for the both of us. I didn't hear from her at all for about a month, but often thought of her. She had gotten to me more than I would have liked to admit. Under all my nonchalance, I really did wish we were still dating, but knew where she stood and wasn't ever planning on pushing the issue.

Until things *did* change.

Unexpectedly, she called me up one Tuesday night, and at the end of the conversation she admitted her lingering feelings.

"I miss you," she said. "I think you should come down for the weekend. Do you want to?"

Now at this juncture, the voices of reason in the back of my head wanted me to ask if there were any vacant rooms in the emotional hotel accommodations of her heart. What was the availability status, I wondered? And how was the room service? But I was afraid to ruin the moment and the weekend with such an inquisition, so I simply responded, "Sure. I'd like that."

Against my better judgment, I was going to spend a full 48 hours with a girl I was crazy about—who didn't just give me butterflies, but butterfly knives in my gut—who for all intents and purposes still did not want to "explore these feelings" she had. So I did what any lovesick chump would do in my shoes. I promised myself to spend the whole weekend being so rad that she wouldn't be able to help but want to go exploring.

We set plans and talked the remainder of the week until Friday came around, sharing our mutual excitement to see one another and what we were going to do the whole weekend.

"I was thinking we'd go out for sushi Friday night when you get here, and then we can just hang out with my roommates and their boyfriends afterward. Saturday, I thought we could go play soccer." She knew her playing soccer turned me on something fierce. "And then later, my friends and I thought it would be great to go to this dinner theatre show called *Lips*."

"Sounds great," I replied. The weekend was going to be perfect, I thought.

"What kind of dinner theatre is it?" I was curious.

"It's a drag show."

"Oh...well that's...fun." At that moment, my common sense packed its bags, said so long, and took off for some uncharted exotic island thousands of miles away.

I didn't know when or if I'd see it again.

***

Lips was indeed a drag show, as flamboyant as they come, with a very laissez-faire definition of classy entertainment that at times bordered on downright debauchery. It was something straight from the film *The Birdcage*; I expected Nathan Lane to sashay in at any minute. Every server was a drag queen impersonating his favorite diva. Our server was a Mexican Liza Minnelli, who oddly enough reminded me a lot of my own mother. The hostess of the show was a stunning Cher (circa "If I Could Turn Back Time") and she emceed the night's entertainment—various song and dance numbers put on by elaborately done up cross-dressers.

I would find out that the joke Mandy had pulled was that she told the Man-Cher that it was my birthday, and that I had a very good sense of humor and would easily feel comfortable being publicly embarrassed. However, only one of these two statements was true, and if Man-Cher had paid more attention to my driver's license when she carded me, she would have realized Mandy was full of shit and just wanted to put me in the hot seat—literally.

After I confessed to never having had a lap dance, Man-Cher led me to the center of the stage and sat me down in a chair.

"Well, don't worry, baby," she said. "After tonight, you will. Your friend Mandy was a doll and told us it was your birthday, and this is what you wished for."

"Did she?" I asked, shooting Mandy a dirty look.

"Yes. And we here at *Lips* have something very special planned for your special day."

The audience—a generous number of eager onlookers—whistled and catcalled, and Mandy sat there amongst them with her sly grin, waiting for the show to start. As the stage lights went dark, I remembered my commitment to being colossally rad in front of Mandy, so I promised myself that whatever was to come next, I was going to own it and become a drag show star.

The spotlight came down on me and the music began. As the front lights came up, out from the wings came a cowgirl who, under her chaps, was definitely packing heat. She, a manly Shania Twain, heehawed onto the stage to the song "Man! I Feel Like a Woman!", though later, when she bounced up and down on my lap, she certainly didn't.

She playfully danced around me, and I just hammed it up and danced along with her in my seat. She seemed amused by my willingness, and then directed her attention to my shirt's buttons. One by one she unbuttoned them, removed my shirt, and then threw it to the crowd. There was thunderous applause. I, too stubborn to show any signs of apprehension, didn't miss a beat and rubbed my bare chest. To me, it was a battle of wills—to see who was going to break first, outgunned and outqueered by the other. I was going to take no prisoners. But apparently she was, because she brought out handcuffs.

So there I was, handcuffed to a chair, completely at the mercy of Man-Shania. She straddled me and rode me like a young buck that needed to be broken in. At this point, I realized if there was ever any question in regards to my sexual orientation, it had now been answered—I was not a big fan of our junk smashing together. After the grinding of man parts, she proceeded to unzip my pants just a notch. This seemed to be getting a little out of hand, and at this point I'm sure I showed a little worry on my face. One of the wait staff suddenly appeared with some Reddi-wip and handed it to my jailer. Man-Shania then proceeded to lather a giant arrow pointing down my chest and stomach.

"Okay. This by definition is no longer a lap dance," I thought, and was uncertain what was going to happen next.

"Are you ready for your birthday surprise?" the cowgirl asked in a Southern baritone drawl.

"Uh, wasn't the lap dance the surprise?"

"Not exactly." She cooed. And with this, she pulled off her bandana and blindfolded me. The crowd started singing "Happy Birthday" and I could hear all sorts of giggling. When the song was finished, they removed the blindfold and had Mandy up on stage too. They kneeled her down in front of the lathered whipped-cream mess and shoved her face in it.

I was happy my humiliation wasn't a solo act.

"Thank you for being a good sport," Mandy said, after we had both washed up. "Here's your shirt back, though you should keep it off."

What did this mean? All weekend, nothing besides some harmless flirting had occurred between us, and I wondered if this suggested things might get more a little more heated when we got back to her apartment. Was she really *that* turned on by watching me get a lap dance from a drag queen? Do they even have a name for girls like that? The answer wasn't important, or so I thought.

Later that evening, Mandy, her roommates and I played a drunken game of Truth or Dare that began with my being dared to run through Mandy's apartment complex in only my boxers screaming, "I like Mandy," and concluded with her and me locked in a closet, doing exactly what drunken people do in closets—a whole lot of sloppy making out. Afterward, Mandy led me up to the bedroom, and we continued our makeout session in her bed.

But before things got any more heated, she stopped suddenly, looked me dead straight in the eyes, and said, "I want to do something."

"What?" I asked.

"Hold on." She paused from kissing me and reached over to her bedside drawer, opened and sifted through it.

My imagination was spinning, or maybe it was just my head from the alcohol, but I was pretty certain I knew what she was going to pull out and started pulling down my pants. I was surprised when, in her hands, she presented a fuzzy pair of purple handcuffs.

"I want to use these. I want to tie you up and do things to you, and I don't want you to be able to do anything at all—even kiss me," she said.

I was befuddled. This was not what I expected, and a little too kinky to consider doing with a girl I had such sincere feelings for.

I'd like to say that I kissed her on her cheek, told her I was tired and turned over to go to sleep.

But I can't.

I was drunk on her and too much whiskey, and as I have already established, had no common sense where she was concerned.

***

The following morning, I awoke to the kind of moment of clarity that comes only after hitting the very bottom of one's own moral fiber. Everything became clear about Mandy and the kind of girl she was, why she bailed when we first started dating, and why she insisted on putting me in situations where I was always tied up. A control freak, she couldn't handle the possibility of letting go of her own heart.

I wanted to dare Mandy to run through her apartment complex shouting. I wanted to dare her to embarrass herself for someone else. I wanted to dare her common sense to go on vacation along with mine and send us photographs of beaches and sunsets.

I never did. My own common sense returned to me and I left for Long Beach with it in tow. Mandy hasn't made my heart kick since.

BRASS KNUCKLES

"Next," Ashley calls out from behind the Walgreens counter, looking as entertained as a four-year-old at a physics lecture. There are two people in line ahead of me.

I stop in Walgreens every Friday afternoon, because to the best of my knowledge, that is the shift Ashley most consistently works. I've seen her stocking shelves on Wednesday mornings, working the register late Sunday nights, and once on Christmas Eve I bumped into her while crossing the corner of the frozen food aisle. I was buying frozen peas. I dropped them and she dropped a bottle of Windex. I tried apologizing with the kind of inarticulate finesse often associated with secret admirers or the disabled, and mustered a polite "Maaaaah." She growled and walked away—the sway of her hips in perfect unison to the blue liquid swishing around the clear plastic container in her hand.

But on Fridays she's always here. And so am I, each week finding anything to fill a basket, pretending I'm just any other customer picking up his weekend necessities—paper towels, dish soap, bologna, pop tarts, and condoms. Every Friday I buy a pack of condoms to give the illusion I'm sexually active—that I'm wild and in heat. I'm not, momentarily. I've been before. Twice. Needless to say there are a lot of unopened condom packages in my bedside drawer.

"Next!" Ashley says again, this time sounding annoyed. The old man at the front of the line looks confused, picks at the hearing aid in his ear, and walks towards the register. His pants are too short and his mismatched socks—one navy blue, the other argyle—scream for attention. I feel bad for him and wonder if his lack of fashion sense is a reflection of sock shortage or the onset of dementia.

"What do you want?" He points at something behind her and leans in really close so none of us in line can make out what he's saying. Turns out, neither can Ashley.

"I'm sorry dude, I can't hear you." Ashley's apology is more sharp than sincere. He whispers again, gesturing with shaky hands for her to slouch forward so he can be discreet.

"Oh. Gotcha."

Ashley turns around. I am standing far enough away that I can see her rear from over the countertop, and can make out the lines of her panties—little boy shorts, probably lacy and black—under the khakis she wears tighter than Walgreens would probably like. This kills me.

She sifts through all the adult magazines kept behind the register along with the expensive booze, nicotine gum, cough syrup and Pedialyte.

"Which mag was it again?" she asks nonchalantly, like she's inquiring about his favorite color. "The one with the fat chicks, right?" The plus-sized woman in front of me is not amused.

Ashley looks over her shoulder at the man for confirmation. He nods. She rings him up and puts his shame in a brown paper bag.

The woman in front of me, heavy set and wearing a muumuu, takes her turn and walks up to Ashley.

"I'd like some ice cream, please." As soon as she says this I can just see the judgments swirling in Ashley's head. She tries to keep face, but her hazel eyes betray her. Her pupils are ninjas—silent lethal killers—and they shoot daggers at her.

"All right." Ashley is biting her tongue. She walks over to the ice cream case and lifts the glass. "What flavor?"

"Mint chocolate chip," muumuu lady responds. "Two scoops, please."

I can hear Ashley mutter, "Really?" under her breath. So does the woman.

"What?"

"Oh. Nothing." Ashley grabs a cone and is about to scoop, but is interrupted.

"Not *that* kind. The other one *please*. If I *wanted* sugar-free I would have asked for it." She glares at Ashley, and I'm afraid the lady is going to eat her.

"Here. That will be a dollar eighty-nine. Thank you. Bye."

When it's my turn to pay, I avoid eye contact at all costs, afraid that if our eyes lock she'll be able to read my thoughts and will know how I want her—how I think she's the most dangerous beauty I have ever known. I see how she treats customers, and imagine that her harshness belies a wild spirit unafraid to say and do anything she wants. I bet she carries brass knuckles in her purse.

"Big night tonight?" she says, holding up the two boxes of Durex condoms.

"Huh? Oh. I have a coupon. Um. Buy one get one free." She smells of cigarettes and cinnamon gum, and she makes me nervous. I wonder if she notices the stutter in my voice or my sweaty palm as I hand her the coupon.

She rings up my condoms, eggs, *Men's Health Magazine* and turkey bacon like she's never seen me before. I'm not sure if this is comforting or upsetting.

"$19.30."

"Here." I hand her my card to swipe and she prints out a receipt for me to sign. My fingers feel numb. In theory, it would be so easy for me to write my number on the back of this little piece of white paper. After eight months it shouldn't be this difficult to make a move, any move. But it is. She scares and excites me. She just got a new tattoo; it reads 'book' on her left hand's knuckles and 'worm' on her right.

I chicken-scratch my name and give her back the sales slip. Our fingers touch briefly and this is the highlight of my week. Her nails are painted cobalt blue, and are chipping. She bites them. I've never wanted to be fingernails more badly in my life.

"Thank you," I say. "Have a great weekend." I've been practicing saying this in my head for the past ten minutes to make sure I didn't stumble over my words.

"Thanks. You too." She lets her lips curl ever so slightly into a smile I could slit my wrists with. Damn, she is beautiful.

***

"So she's beautiful? Big fucking deal, Matt. Grow a pair," Brad says, before finishing the last of his beer. He points the empty bottle head in my direction and calls me a pussy.

"Your round, pussy."

Brad and I have a deal that any time I bring up Ashley, I owe him a drink.

"Right. Back in a sec." I get up from the table and go over to the bar for two more Heinekens. Brad's tone doesn't much surprise me— he's had to listen to my pining for this girl for months now. At first he was great about the whole thing and really tried to offer advice—how I could ask her out, assuring me that I *should* ask her out.

"We're just way too different. She'd never be interested in me," I had said the first time I told him about Ashley.

"So?" was his response. "Opposites attract and all that shit. Obviously, or else you wouldn't be so hot for the girl. Maybe deep down, she's been waiting for boring ol' you to come into her life and ask her out."

"Funny. I'm not *that* boring."

"Matt, I love ya man, but you are. The last first date you went on, you had tea and played Scrabble. My grandfather gets further on dates than you, and he's in a fucking wheelchair."

"So I take things slow."

"Natural selection takes things *slow*. You redefine the word entirely. Have you ever even kissed a girl on the first date?" Brad asked.

"No."

"Well, that explains why the girls you do end up with are probably left baffled as to whether or not they've actually been on a date with you. Seriously, man, take a plunge into the deep end." Brad has been singing this same song, different verse to me now probably close to a hundred times—he's right to lose his patience with me.

As I make my way back to our table with the beers, I see him texting, no doubt probably trying to find some piece of ass for the night. There was a time when he was just as clueless about girls as I was—when we'd spend our weekly allowance on candy and comic books from the corner liquor store, staying up all night watching and re-watching *The Empire Strikes Back*—but he grew out of thirteen a lot faster than I did. By summer's end before we started high school, Brad had a few things I still wouldn't until well after our senior year—sprouts of chest hair, a girlfriend and his first hand job. Now, years later, chatting up women comes easy to him, like breathing or masturbating, while I, on the other hand, am just slightly less hopeless than my adolescent self.

"Thanks." Brad looks up at me and takes one of the bottles from my hand.

"Sure," I say.

He puts his phone away, leans back in his chair and stretches. I sit down and nurse my fifth beer.

"So who were ya texting?" I ask.

"Some girl I met last night while I was bartending. Going to see if she's free later."

"That job is the best thing to ever happen to your sex life," I tell him.

"What? You mean hot chicks don't just hand out their numbers to you at the comic book store?"

"Sadly no. They seem to flock to your place of employment a lot more than they do mine."

"Wasn't there that one? What was her name again?" Brad asks.

"Ann. But it would have never worked out; she was a huge DC fan."

Brad calls me a geek, I call him a tool, we laugh, but he can see I'm still in my head.

"Seriously, man. Just ask Ashley out already. The longer you don't say anything, the longer she'll just think you're some freaky stalker creep."

"Come on, man, no…I only go there on Fridays. It's perfectly normal for someone to pick up groceries the same day every week."

"Uh-huh. The same day for eight months straight?" Brad asks.

"Yeah."

"What about the long stares?"

"I try to keep those to a minimum."

"Look," Brad starts in, "I've said this before. I'm probably going to have to say it again—but whatever, man. What's the fucking worst that can happen if you ask her out? She says no and you stop shopping at Walgreens. Boo-fucking-hoo."

"I'm more afraid of her saying *yes* than no."

"I get that. I do. But after all this time, you have to have built up enough nerve to find out for certain. You owe that to yourself. And God dammit, you owe it to me."

"You're right. I know. We'll see," I say.

I take a final swig from my Heineken and, smirking, push the empty green bottle on the table towards Brad.

"I'll take another," I tell him.

"Huh?"

"Technically, you brought her up that time."

Before getting up to get us two more beers, Brad grins and says, "You're going to be all right, Matt." And just then I know he's right; in the end, I *am* going to be all right.

***

"I'm open over here." Ashley waves me over to her register. She's dyed her hair since last week—it's darker, more plum in color than her usual red.

I've been thinking a lot about what Brad said to me at the bar last Friday night—how I do owe it to myself, after all this time, to find out for certain what Ashley would say if I asked her out. And he does kind of have a point; if I don't do anything about these feelings and come out of the shadows, I'm no better than some weirdo with a crush. That ends tonight. Tonight I find my balls.

I walk up to Ashley and put two items on her check stand counter, a bouquet of lilacs and half a pint of Jack Daniel's—for courage. Not wanting to make things awkward for us in front of the customers and other employees, I decide it best to wait for her in the parking lot until she gets off work.

As she rings up the flowers, I'm excited by the thought of giving them to her later. She puts them in a plastic bag, careful to not disrupt their light purple petals, and sheaths the bottle of Jack in a miniature paper bag. I am almost giddy.

"Thanks," I say, handing her the money. I consciously choose to pay by cash, because I imagine my hand would tremble too much if I attempted to sign a credit receipt.

"You're welcome," she says. She looks tired. I'm not certain what time she started work tonight, but it's a little before nine now. At the latest, she'll be out some time after eleven when they close. I smile, take my flowers and whiskey from her, and make my way to the parking lot to wait. The automatic glass doors part, and as I walk out of them, I can feel the crisp fall night air tingle my cheeks. I open my little bottle of whiskey and take my first sip. The smooth charcoal finish instantly warms me, along with thoughts of things to come. My head is full of fantasies for the next two hours as I imagine how the conversation will go. I get drunk off of Jack and wishful thinking.

Half past eleven, I notice employees starting to trickle out of the store, making their way to their cars. I quickly toss the empty bottle aside and grab the flowers from the passenger seat. I wait but I don't see her right away.

Finally, she makes her way out and lights a cigarette; the flame from her lighter makes her face glow orange like a jack o' lantern. As she heads towards a group of cars where hers is most likely parked, I make a beeline for her from across the lot.

"Um. Hi, Ashley," I say.

"How do you know my name?" She hurls this question at me like a boulder and catches me off guard.

"Uh…your nametag. I…um…thought we could…I mean I wanted you to…well if we could just…my number—"

"Look, asshole," she cuts me off, "I don't know who you think you are coming in here every week making goddamn googly-eyes at me and always buying condoms, but get a fucking life."

"But I was just…" I try to get a word in, but she clearly isn't interested in listening as she interrupts me again.

"Fuck off, creep." She walks past me, giving me her back and the middle finger.

"Wait, these are for you." I almost completely forget about the lilacs I am still holding onto like they were my last shreds of dignity. I go to grab her shoulder to get her attention, but she quickly turns to face me, pulling something from her purse. Before I realize what it is, my eyes swell with tears, I begin coughing uncontrollably, and my face feels as if it's on fire.

Pepper spray? Pepper spray? *Really?*

My body spasms so violently that I can't bear to stand and fall to the ground. I can't see anything, but sense Ashley is near.

"Stay out of the store, asshole!" She crushes the flowers under the sole of her Converse—I hear the plastic around them rustle between rubber and asphalt before she stomps off into the distance, leaving me curled up into a heaving, coughing ball. I'm coughing so much now the whiskey in my gut starts to make me even sicker, and I vomit off to my side.

I lie there next to the crumpled lilacs, crying, with the taste of vomit in my mouth, and the realization that all I ever was to her was just another nut job she got paid to put up with every week—*the condom guy.*

If this is what taking a plunge into the deep end feels like, forget it.

THE REUNION

"Can I get a Jack on the rocks?" I ask the bartender while checking my phone's messages, hoping to look more important than I feel. I watch her pour my drink over a glacier of ice. I'll have to remember this. Watered-down booze is not going to help me survive my high school reunion; I'll have to order my next whiskey neat.

She hands me my drink. I start to thank her, but am interrupted by a booming voice behind me.

"Hey, shit socks!"

I do nothing but sit and pretend I'm someone else, hoping they will think they have the wrong guy.

"SHIT SOCKS!"

No such luck.

I smile to my cute bartender; embarrassed by the nickname I've longed to forget. I know who it is before I even turn around. Bryant DeWolf—valedictorian, track star, lead in all the school plays, and total asshole.

"I knew it was you, shit socks! How the hell have ya been?" I hesitate a moment to give the impression I don't remember him, to screw with his ego some.

"Good...*um*...Bryant. Good." My second "good" hangs in the air like a corpse. I don't ask how he is.

"*Man, ten years, huh*? What have ya been up to?" he asks.

Bryant looks about the same, still built like a Roman statue—that bastard. However, there are now dark circles under his blue eyes, his teeth are yellowed from smoking, and his jet-black hair has begun to recede noticeably. This makes me happy; hereditary male baldness does not run in my family, and I'll take whatever victory, regardless how small, I can on this night. The left side of his face also looks a little swollen and puffy.

"I'm an artist," I tell him—hesitantly. "I draw."

"Cool, man. What do ya draw?"

God dammit, I think to myself. *When the hell did Bryant ever care so much about me?* This officially has become our longest conversation since freshman gym, since before the whole *shit socks* disaster. *Can't he just go be a douche to someone else?* I throw back my whiskey and work a large ice cube around my mouth like a peppermint, savoring its numbing effect against the inside of my cheek. The DJ tries to entice us all to come to the dance floor for a slow song. Celine Dion's "My

Heart Will Go On" begins to play. I want to open a vein.

I settle for crunching ice under my molars instead.

"Comic books," I say.

"Really?" he asks, chuckling a little, not even looking me straight in the face.

"Yeah. Really."

"I'm sorry, it's just…I mean…I remember you always doodling in class…superheroes and shit. You make a living at it now?"

"I do all right."

"That's good man…I mean, great." He's trying to be sincere. I attempt a little of the same.

"What about you?" I ask, almost expecting his answer to be something like lawyer, brain surgeon or firefighter—maybe a combination of all three.

"I took over my father's business," he says.

After a few seconds of silence, I ask, "Wasn't your dad a mortician?"

"Yeah."

"Wow. What's that like?"

"*I see dead people…*hah."

I don't laugh.

"No, seriously, it's a good business, even with the economy—people are always dying," he jokes.

"I guess." I laugh a little now—not with him, but at him.

I gesture to the bartender for another drink and order a whiskey, neat. She asks Bryant what he'd like.

"An MGD for me and two Coronas for my buddies," he says, pointing at the two talking at a small table behind us. I don't entirely recognize them, nor care to. She reaches under the bar, pulls out three bottles, and then gives me a generous pour of Jack.

"I've got it," Bryant says as he pulls out a fifty-dollar bill and waves it at the bartender, wide-grinned and yellow-toothed. And just like that, I hate him again.

"Thanks," I say. It's little restitution for sticking me with a nickname like *shit socks*, but it's probably all the amends he has in him to make.

"No problem, dude," Bryant says, slapping me on the back as if we're old chums. He turns around to hand his two friends their beer. They've been too busy in their own nostalgia, no doubt, to see that Bryant and I are the best of friends now. I think one of them was our homecoming king, Chad Garret. But if it is, the only royalty he's running for now is Burger King—he's pushing well over three hundred pounds. Another notch in the win column for me.

"Hey, it's been great catching up," Bryant says, bringing the cold beer up to his face and pressing it against his swollen left cheek, "but we're going to go see if we can't find Heather Collins. Remember her? She had her belly button pierced sophomore year...man...she was hot. She was one of the first girls to do that. I heard she married The Buckmaster, and they have six kids now. Six. Can you believe it?"

"Wow," I say.

"Yeah, they're Mormon. She converted for him. I want to see if she's still got that body."

"That's great." I'm lying. I could care less. "Tell them both *shit socks* says hello."

"Hah! I will, Dave." My own name sounds strange coming out of Bryant's mouth.

"Good luck with the whole dead people thing," I say.

"Hah. Yeah," he chuckles. "And good luck to you and your superheroes, man."

"Thanks."

Bryant begins to walk away, but then turns abruptly. "Hey, have you seen your buddy Jim?"

Jim, my best friend from middle and high school, and I fell out of touch after our first couple semesters away at college. We'd call here and there, but eventually lost track of one another. Last we spoke was when I heard his mom was diagnosed with lung cancer. That was over four years ago, and we haven't talked since. Eventually, phone numbers and email addresses changed, and before I knew it we were ghosts in each other's lives.

I had wondered if he was going to make it to the reunion—seeing him was the only reason I'd decided to come.

"No. Why?" I ask. "Have you?"

"Just wondering. See ya around, man," Bryant says, smirking.

"See you."

As Bryant takes off to revisit the past with all of the other ten-years-later versions of our school's once privileged and popular, I decide to revisit the cute bartender. I quickly finish the drink Bryant bought me so I can order another and do a little flirting. Back in high school, I wouldn't have had the guts to even talk to a girl like her. Too shy, I would instead sit in class longing for the ones I had crushes on, sketching their likenesses again and again on pages of lined notebook paper.

I will often get asked by fans of my artwork where I learned to pay so much attention to the line and curvature of the female form; they laugh when I tell them Junior AP English. I remember that class particularly well—I sat a row across from Courtney Hobbs. I must have drawn her hundreds of times in the margins of my notes over the course of that year, though I never dared show her. I never showed anyone, except Jim.

I could always confide in Jim the girls I wished I was not too shy to talk to, too lowly to ask out. He'd even try convincing me to man up and say fuck it to the whole she's-out-of-my-league mentality. I can still recall the best advice he ever tried to give me: "So what if Courtney is a cheerleader, Dave? She takes a shit like everyone else."

Jim was brave like that—a real natural when it came to the ladies, he could chat up any girl without breaking a sweat. I wish he could see me flirt now, with the balls I bet he always wanted me to have back then.

"Can I get another, *sweetheart*?" I ask the bartender using the endearment like a harpoon, hoping it would catch.

"Sure," she smiles. I'm not certain if it's one of those because-she's-interested smiles, or those it's-her-job-to-be-nice-and-appear-interested smiles. Either way, I'm happy to sit here, drink and find out.

Her freckles glow under the dim light above the bar. She looks at me, cocks an eyebrow and asks, "Why'd that guy call you *shit socks*? Did you wipe your ass with your socks or something?"

She just killed the mood.

"Long story," I say. "I have to piss. I'll tell you when I get back."

I am not coming back.

***

I get knocked down, but I get up again, Chumbawamba sings over the bathroom's speakers as I am taking a leak. Just above the urinal, a framed advertisement for chewing tobacco is staring me in the face. I see my reflection in the glass and can't help but think I don't look all that different. I wonder if that's what it's like for everyone here. Do they see themselves as they always were, regardless of how they've changed—how much hair's been lost, or how much weight's been gained? And while some desperately cling to visages of the past, there are those of us who want nothing more than to bury that person we were in high school.

This was a mistake. If I haven't bumped into Jim yet, then he's not here and I'm sticking around for nothing. I zip up, wash my hands, and with curiosity satiated, make up my mind that I am leaving. Goodbye, class of '98. I won't be seeing you in another ten.

***

Standing in the parking lot, waiting for a cab, I am approached by an unfamiliar, husky woman wearing a red cocktail dress a few sizes too small. Her feet are enormous, and I am surprised she's found stilettos her size. She is smoking, and takes the cigarette hanging like a broken diving board on her lower lip between two long fingers and blows a cloud of smoke from her flaring nostrils before she says, "Dave?"

"Uh...hello. Do I know you?" I say, thinking there is something about her voice I can't place, but am certain I've heard before.

"It's me. Jim. Well...I go by Jane now," she says, unabashed, like it's a self-declaration she's had to make over a thousand times now, and has practiced even more. Slack-jawed, I look carefully at her like I'm examining an old photograph; underneath all the makeup—the eye shadow, lipstick, blush and foundation—I see the face of my old, dear friend.

"Holy fucking Christ! What the fuck, Jim?"

"It's Jane, Dave."

"What?!"

"I realize this is a bit shocking. We haven't talked in a real long time."

"No shit."

"I'm sorry. I should have gotten in touch with you—should have told you. Sorry. I just didn't know what to say, how to tell *you* of all people."

"No, it's cool. I mean, just a bit of a punch in the gut."

"I know, I know. I had no idea in high school. I mean, I always felt kind of different—weird. But I had no clue really. Does that sound strange?" she asks.

"Yes. No. I don't know."

Whatever buzz I had is gone now, and I am more confused than I have been in a really long time. Memories of our adolescence begin to flash in my head, and one particular memory hits me with a whole new context. In seventh grade, my mother bought the incredibly inappropriate guidebook to puberty, *What is Happening to My Boy's Body?* I remember the chapter on masturbation being horribly awkward; it compared semen to Gatorade for sperm, declared that

54

coaches encourage their players to stroke it before a big game to relieve tension, and that it wasn't uncommon for young boys to beat each other off rather than masturbate themselves—advocating this wasn't to be considered gay at all.

My mother gave a copy of the book to Jim's mom, and Jim read the book as well. One day after school while playing video games, Jim referred to the book, specifically the chapter on boys masturbating, and asked if I had read it. Not diverting my attention away from the TV screen to make eye contact, I just said, "Uh-huh." I could feel Jim's eyes on me when he asked if we could "masturbate each other," that, "the book said it wasn't gay." I paused the game, looked at him, and said, "Yeah…I think it is," and returned to zapping spaceships. We never talked about it or the book again.

"So…um, are you like…gay," I ask her, "or do you just feel…um, more comfortable in drag?"

"I'm not gay," she says with a tiny laugh.

"So you like chicks?"

"No. I like men."

"But…" She cuts me off before I say something stupid.

"I'm a woman, Dave. It's just for most of my life I was in the wrong skin."

"That's cool." I search for what to say next. "So…um…when did you know?"

"College. At first, I thought it was just experimentation. I started hooking up with guys, but still felt really confused." This is difficult to hear; it is hard to imagine my best friend, Jim, rolling around in a dorm room bed of some frat guy. Imagining Jane doing so as she is in front of me now, however, comes a little easier.

"Being with a guy felt right enough to me," Jane continues to explain, "but something about myself was still all wrong." She tosses the cigarette she's finished smoking to the pavement and puts it out under the heel of her stiletto, doing so naturally, as if she's been wearing heels her entire life. I look down at her chubby feet, covered in nylon, strapped and swelling in a glossy black slipper like some drag queen Cinderella-hooker. I notice the lush magenta stain of her lipstick on the butt of the cigarette lying dead now on the asphalt. There is something both trashy and elegant about her.

"Why didn't you ever tell me?" I ask her. "You know I would have been cool with it. It wouldn't have been a big deal, you know?"

"Yes and no. The reason I never said anything was because I realized I always had this *huge* crush on you." The confidence Jane

55

exuded only moments ago is slowly dissipating. "It was really hard for me to come to terms with my feelings and all the memories. I guess I was being selfish keeping you in the dark about the whole thing. I was just afraid that if I told you, it would completely change the past, you know, make the friendship seem like it was always about something else."

"Was it?" I ask, afraid of what her answer might be.

"I don't know. I'm sorry. After all this time, I'm not sure if I can trust my memories—I don't really know if things were as I remember them, or if this secret was always just below the surface," Jane says.

"Well, if it's any proof things are the same, they're still calling me *shit socks*," I say, trying to break the tension.

Jane's goofy smile screams back to Jim and our adolescence—stealing quarters from our mothers' purses for the arcade, hours spent each week at the comic book store, and every argument we ever had over which superpower would be more badass to have in real life—and for a brief moment it feels like nothing's changed, but things have. They've changed more between us in the last few minutes than in ten years of an absent friendship.

"They called you *that* tonight?"

"Bryant DeWolf did."

"Bryant's a corpse fucker," Jane says, and I laugh.

"You saw him tonight, I take it?"

"Yeah. He was a jerk. Made some really shitty comments. Said I looked slutty. I asked if he wanted a blowjob, and he swung at me. He missed and I gave him a good right cross to his left."

I'm still laughing, partly at the mental image of Bryant screwing cadavers, and partly at the thought of him being punched in the face by my now-transgender best friend in a cocktail dress, black stilettos, and a Louis Vuitton handbag draping from her shoulder.

"I mean, can't a lady look sexy without suggesting she's a ho'?" Jane jokes, lighting another cigarette.

"When did you start...I mean, why did you...do you..."

"You're wondering if I still have my junk," she interrupts, but yes, this is exactly what I am trying to say.

Back when we were twelve, Jim and I had found a stash of pornography thrown out in the alley behind his condominium. We snuck them back to his room and spent hours studying the variety of women, poses and sexual acts. One of the magazines featured a section of "she-males," and I quickly tossed it aside, disgusted. I remember Jim, however, was "intrigued by their freakishness," he had said. I didn't really think much of it then—thought he meant it in the same vein as people do who slow down at the scene of an automobile accident, hoping to see something brutal and shocking. I had never imagined there was more to it than that.

"Yes. I'm pre-op," she tells me. "I'm on all the hormones and undergoing the psych evaluations; once the year is over and all the finances go through, I'll have the procedure done."

"That's intense, man." I catch myself. "Sorry."

"It's all right."

"When did you figure all this out, that this is what you wanted?"

"Back when my mom was first diagnosed," Jane says. "She wanted me to know in case something went wrong."

"Know what?" I ask.

"That I was born with both parts," she says, and I can see how difficult this is for her. "My folks and the doctors had to make a choice. Apparently they chose wrong. After she passed, I decided to put what was left of her estate and life insurance towards the procedure. I think she would have wanted me to."

"I'm so sorry."

"No, it's okay."

"Look…I was going to get out of here, but if you want, we could go someplace and talk more." I suggest this, imagining it's the right thing to do after my estranged best friend and I have a five-minute catch-up, where I learn he's a pre-op transgender who may or may not have had a crush on me growing up. Unlike puberty, this sort of thing isn't covered in any guidebooks.

Jane takes a long drag from her cigarette then, flicking away its ashes, looks at me like I'm some kind of stranger.

"No. That's all right. Thank you, though. I'm going to go back inside and see the rest of the freak show. Seriously, though…thanks."

We don't hug. We don't shake hands. We just wave across the distance between us and say goodbye.

As I'm about to turn and hail a cab, Jane makes one last joke, telling me how in another ten years she'll have a vagina, and then things will be even weirder. She smiles that goofy smile, puts out her cigarette and walks away without looking back, leaving me to face forward in a direction I'm not entirely sure of.

PERMANENCE

I am staring into the glassy yellow eye of a dinosaur off the 10 Freeway on the way to Palm Desert, anxious for what comes next. My girlfriend, Megan, is beside me taking video of its clunky, robotic movements—its head turning and body twisting from left to right like a mechanical Santa in a department store window. I am both amused and disappointed by how fake the creature in front of us is, and ask her if she's ready to go.

"If you are, sure." Her dyed-red hair blows in her face as she says this. Strands get caught in her mouth before she can say anything else, and I assume the wind is getting a bit much for her.

"It won't be this windy at my folks'. It's always heavy here. That's why there's all those windmills." I wave my hand in the air, referencing the wall of them we passed a few miles back before we stopped to see the dinosaurs.

"It's fine," she says, smiling, and I *know* it is with her. I know she doesn't really mind her hair messed up, that she's not nervous to meet my parents, and that seeing my mother's illness isn't going to rattle her, isn't going to make her numb and knotted inside the way it does me.

Walking back to the car she asks, "Is it as you remembered it, this place, from when you were a kid?"

"No," I say pointing up at the giant Tyrannosaurus' disproportionate pear-shaped belly. "They have really let themselves go."

Megan laughs the kind of laugh a girlfriend gives when her man says something dumb trying to be clever, and then takes my hand.

"How far are your parents from here?"

"About thirty minutes. We should be there by four."

"Sounds good," she says, squeezing my hand—our palms so flush against each other now, I imagine we become one.

***

"So what do the doctors think it is now?" I had asked my father on the phone a week ago. "Hashi-what? Mom tried to explain to me. Something about swelling in her brain, but she was getting a little mixed up."

"It's called Hashimoto's Encephalopathy. It's pretty rare and often goes misdiagnosed since it resembles a number of neurological disorders. But they are fairly positive this is what it is." My father's response sounded so clinical, as if he'd read and reread the research material enough times now so the jargon comes fluidly.

"But, what is it exactly? Is it her brain, then?"

"It's onset by her thyroid affecting her brain, altering its functioning—it's causing... basically a swelling, which is responsible for all her symptoms: the dementia and memory loss, trouble concentrating, difficulty speaking and walking."

"Is it...it's curable, right? Mom said something about treatment."

"It's not curable, but is treatable. With steroids and an infusion, it should bring her back to normal. We'll just have to keep an eye on her in the future."

"And the doctors...they seem sure this time? And you feel confident they're right?" I had asked, knowing what aggravation they've endured having carrots dangled in front of them time and time again.

"Yeah, this new neurologist she's got has seen it before, and he's compared all the results from every test she's had done. He feels it's substantiated."

"Well, that's good, then."

"She's really excited for Saturday. She's cleaned the house twice this week already, and has the maids scheduled to come out that afternoon."

"Good. I'm looking forward to it as well, for the two you to meet Megan."

"Kevin, try to be patient with your mother, okay?"

"Yes, Dad, I know. I will be."

***

My mother greets us with a smile that says she's been looking forward to our visit all week. She's gained some weight, which is good; the last time I saw her, she was bones and skin, hardly any fat and far less muscle. But for this small, much welcomed improvement, there are also new symptoms of the disease springing to life and striking at her body—some visible, others painstakingly not. The right side of her face hangs loose, like a timepiece in a Salvador Dali painting; her right eyelid droops and her cheek sags as she says hello. I try hard not to let my mother see how unfamiliar she looks to me like this.

"Mom, this is Megan."

"Hi," Megan says warmly. My mother goes to hug her, arms outstretched and shaking. She is weak, but cheerful at the same time, her body struggling.

"Megan, it's so good to meet you. Come in. You're beautiful. Kevin, she's beautiful. Your hair's so red. Are you thirsty? How was the drive?"

My mother is a machine gun of pleasantries and inquisition. It used to get on my nerves—I would want nothing more than to just get through the door without being caught in her line of fire—but now I find it warm, this little piece of my mother, silly with happiness, gone unchanged.

She hurries Megan and me into the kitchen.

"Now, Megan, what would you like to drink?"

"Water's fine, thank you."

"Kevin, would you like anything?"

"No, I'm okay, Mom."

"Megan, Kevin tells me you like *The Golden Girls*! I watch them every day; it's my favorite show!"

"I do. I love it," Megan says. I knew this news would cause my mom to gush, but didn't think it would trump the more obvious, initial questions I'd expect a mother to ask when her son brings home a girl for the first time. Questions about Megan's work, family, or where she's from, I expected; trivia about Betty White I did not.

"Did you know Betty White was originally supposed to play the role of Blanche, not Rose?" Megan tells my mom.

"I had no idea, Megan. Megan, I'm sorry. I hope you don't mind me repeating your name. I just don't want to forget."

"No, no, it's fine," Megan says, rubbing my mother's shoulder, relieving her worry.

"It's just this Hashimoto's. Did Kevin tell you? My brain is swollen. I get confused."

"I told her, Mom. She knows. It's all right."

"I hate it. I am so embarrassed," my mother confesses, trying to keep things straight—clear and focused in her head.

"You don't have to be. I think it's great to finally know what's wrong. Kevin told me it's been over two years you've been in the dark."

"Yes. It's been awful. First they said it was a nerve in my hip, then my thyroid, and then they thought MS. I'm just so tired of this runaround," my mother says, not exaggerating—her mind and body fatigued from wrestling this mystery disease, and her heart, sunken so deep in her chest that any hope offered to her by doctors and specialists now has a hard time reaching it.

"Where's Dad?" I ask.

"He has an open house, I think. He'll be home soon," my mother says, opening the fridge to grab something for herself to drink. As she begins to pour some juice into a glass, she looks at me suspiciously, does not question, but rather states as fact, "You got another tattoo!"

"What?" I say, shocked, unsure if my mom has just forgotten the tattoos I already had when she says this, or if she is utilizing some uncanny mindreading power (something mothers always claim to possess) to know I indeed did get a new tattoo.

"Let me see." With that, I lift up my shirt to show my most recent tattoo sprawled across my ribcage. I can tell she's not thrilled.

"Megan, what do you think of his tattoos?" my mother asks, hoping to gain an ally in her dissatisfaction.

"I don't really mind. I think they're fine," Megan answers, and I'm reminded of our first date. Sitting across from me at a small table, she'd taken my arm and traced her fingers over one of my tattoos, acting curious about them, but really just wanting a reason to touch. The electricity of that first skin-on-skin contact being more permanent than any tattoo ever could.

"Mom, I don't understand why you have such a hard time with them. You have tattoos," I argue.

"I was young."

"You were forty."

"I have a yellow rose on my ankle," she tells Megan, "and a butterfly on my..."

"Mom!" I interrupt, fearing she'll pull down her pants to show us. Megan laughs, but it's happened before.

"You also have your makeup tattooed on," I remind her.

"Oh yes, my eyeliner and eyebrows. It's so nice, but it's not..." she stammers... "*prophylactic*."

"*Prophylactic*?" I ask, not sure if I heard right, and look to Megan to see if she's just as lost.

"Do you mean, *permanent*?" Megan asks, trying to help my mom find the correct word.

"No...*prophylactic*...I have to get them retouched. There's a lady here who does it. When I'm feeling better I'm going...to go..." My mother slows down, realizing she's getting confused. When she gets like this, it's best to let her work through it on her own, else she gets combative, convinced she's making sense.

"I'm sorry. That's not what I meant. Yes, *permanent*…like the marker…they're not permanent. I have to go back in. Kevin, your tattoos aren't permanent, are they? They'll go away eventually, right?"

"No, Mom. They're permanent."

"I mean they'll fade someday," she corrects herself.

"Yeah. Someday," I say, and I guess in her own way, she's right—the ink will bleed and the lines will blur and eventually they won't look anything like they do now.

***

Moving into the living room, my mother walks Megan over to all her framed photos of me as a boy and picks each one up to show her. Megan smiles at her tenderness and I keep silent—browsing magazines on the coffee table, feigning indifference, but secretly enjoying this moment the two of them are sharing.

My mother's show-and-tell is cut short by my father's walking through the front door. "Hello?" he calls out.

"We're in the living room," I say, getting up from the couch to greet him and introduce Megan. "Hi, Dad. This is Megan."

"Hello," he says, shaking her hand.

"Hi, nice to meet you."

"Mom said you were at an open house. How'd it go?" I ask.

"Only one couple came by. Not really a potential buyer."

"I'm sorry."

"It's fine," he says. "How was your drive?"

"Good. We stopped in Cabazon, at the dinosaurs."

"Oh yeah? Megan, had you ever seen them before?" my father asks.

"No. I've driven past them, but have never stopped. They're funny," she says.

"They have a whole attraction there now," I tell him.

"Yeah?"

"Yeah. You pay five bucks and get to see a bunch of outdated animatronic dinosaurs running on their last gears. Megan took some video on her camera. It was pretty ridiculous."

"Did you feel like you went back in time?" my dad asks, trying to be funny.

"Yeah, back to a time of bad production values," she answers, picking up on his humor.

My dad grins and I can already tell she has his approval.

"How are you doing, Cathy?" he turns and asks my mom.

"I feel okay. I ate a whole baked potato for lunch. And half a turkey sandwich."

"That's good," my father says as if praising a small child, proud of her for finishing all her vegetables. But the reality is that her ability to keep food down has been decimated by the ever-changing pills doctors have prescribed.

"Did you take your meds yet?" he asks.

"Yes, right before they got here. Around four."

"Okay. Good. Well, let me just get cleaned up and relax for a bit, and we can head out to dinner by 6?"

"Sure," I say.

"Why don't you show me some more pictures?" Megan asks, and my mom's face lights up like a firecracker.

"Come with me, *Michelle*."

We do not correct her.

***

"This lemon chicken is delicious," Megan says after her first few bites. "You were right, Kevin, this place is really good."

"He makes us come here every time he visits. He has to get his black pepper chicken," my mom teases.

"No place I know makes it this good," I say, wolfing down the peppery meat on my plate, savoring the kick of onion and spice. "How is yours, Mom?"

She looks down at her garlic shrimp. I can tell she wishes she had the appetite to enjoy it more than she does. "It's fine," she says.

"So Megan, Kevin says you're involved in Hollywood?" my dad asks. I am a little surprised by his taking an interest, remembering what I've told him of her. Sometimes I don't think my father listens, but often, he just doesn't ask—and I admit, I can mistake that for his not caring.

"I'm an assistant to a talent manager, yes. It's good. I don't know how much longer I want to stay with it, but it's been good experience, learning the business aspect."

"What do you *want* to do?" he asks, and I'm curious how he will take her answer. My father is all business. Figures and numbers make sense to him. Creativity does not.

"I'd love to direct or produce. I want to tell stories—good stories—

that make people think and feel something different." As she says this, my heart grows fat, but feels so light I'm almost afraid it's going to lift me from my chair and float me towards the ceiling.

"What do you think of what Kevin does? His poetry? Has he dragged you out to watch him?" my father asks, and his use of the word *dragged* does just that—pulls me down.

Seeing this, Megan rests her hand gently on my knee, as if to say, *don't let it.*

"I have," she answers. "He's very good. You've never seen him?" she asks, already knowing the answer.

"No."

"Well, you should sometime."

"Megan's from Carson City," I say quickly, trying to change the subject.

"Did Kevin tell you his brothers were raised in Reno?" he asks, leaving out the fact they are half brothers, from his first marriage.

"Yes, he did. I used to compete for swimming in Reno all the time."

We begin to notice that my mother is keeping strangely quiet. Her eyes are open, but she is far from us.

"Cathy...Cathy." My dad repeats himself.

"Mom...are you okay?" I rest my hand on hers.

"She's been like this for the past few weeks. She goes into this trance-like daze. They're like seizures, only without the shaking, the doctor tells us." My dad says it like it's nothing to worry over.

"What?" I ask, upset I had to find out this way.

"She's probably just too wound up. She hasn't let herself relax all day."

"Mom," I say again, not wanting to talk as if she's not sitting there next to us—like she's not there at all.

"Yes," she says, finally coming around, unaware of what's just happened.

"Are you all right, Cathy?" my dad asks.

"...Yes...except..."

She's stumbling. Slurring.

"Well... Megan hit me in the head with a tennis racket, and then I was so thirsty...I slurped up water from a puppy's dish bowl."

"Cathy, drink some water," my dad tells her, and then turns to us. "She's never been this bad," he says, almost apologizing. And for the first time all night the four of sit silent, looking at each other's faces for answers none have in us to give.

Driving back to LA, it feels as if there's a tornado inside my chest. I look at Megan and I cannot recall ever being this happy and sad all at once—anguished over my mother, yet thankful to know I don't have to carry grief alone anymore.

"Thank you for being with me tonight…for being *you*," I say, meeting her eyes with mine.

She smiles, takes my right hand off the wheel and into hers, resting them on the center console between us.

"When your mom was showing me photos in her bedroom, she told me that you never bring anyone home to meet them."

"No. I don't really."

"Why?"

I shrug to imply I don't have the answer, but do.

I worry I'd be saying too much too soon if I were to confess how I've never wanted to let anyone in so completely before, for fear of things not lasting—how my parents are the drawbridge I use to keep would-be loves from storming the castle of my heart.

"I knew I wanted you to, though," I say, hoping it hints just enough at what's been left unsaid. "I knew it would make my mom happy…to see me happy."

"Thank *you* then, for wanting me to," she says, tracing her fingers along the inside of my palm, and all I can do now is just lose myself to the highway and the slight friction of her touch—ready for what may come.

III

THE REVERBERATION OF LETTING GO

Our naked bodies are tangled strings of Christmas lights.
We are all afterglow and boozy.
Too much red wine in your gut makes you brave
enough to say, *I love*

this song.

I'd forgotten the radio was soundtracking our romance,
wanted instead for the word *you* to escape
from those straitjacket lips,
become visible in the dark
like breath in the cold.

If I could, I'd help it plot its own prison break
from the exercise yard of your throat,
bring it a nail file hidden in a birthday cake,
but I am a terrible baker and you are jellyfish beautiful,

iridescent in the way you move, but dangerous
in how your defenses sting.
I wish you'd drop your guard like a bad habit.
But you warned me,
said you've never been in *love*
as if it were some state you couldn't point to on a map
or a ghost town you weren't even sure existed.

I consider letting the words out right now,
but do not want to play tour guide to your heart.
Rather, I want you to see you're already standing
in front of a welcome sign that reads,
You are here. Population 2.

***

When I said, *I loved Youtube,*
and you shot me a look as if I said something else,
it was sweaty-pits awkward,
erection-in-math-class uncomfortable.

You apologized,
thought you heard the clank
of falling breastplate against floor tile—
the reverberation of letting go.

I fidgeted. Stammered.
Unsure of how to respond to your error—
your maybe hopeful mishearing.

Or perhaps it was my own slip.

Perhaps at that moment, my heart
grew limbs, reached up through my chest
wrestled my tongue into submission, and forced
an utterance of *Uncle* with three words.

But it was that look you gave that lingered.

Your eyes were flare guns, firing brilliant,
as if to signal your exact location, where
you've been clutching a sign of your own
that asked, *What took so long,*

What took so long?

THINGS I'D TELL MY 22-YEAR-OLD SELF
(HAD I ANOTHER TIME MACHINE)

Whatever you're thinking, don't pierce your eyebrow. It will look silly and become infected. Instead, start collecting tattoos. Embrace their permanence. Delight in how your skin sings. Bonus: your mom will hate them.

Keep reading comics. In fact, any girl you date longer than two months, take to a comic book store. If she rolls her eyes more than once, let this be a sign—your spider-sense tingling, to warn you of danger.

Bikini bars are awesome. Dating girls who work at bikini bars is not.

When your parents sell the house you grew up in, keep the key to the front door. Though you'll never use it again, there'll come times you'll want to close a fist around the memory of home.

Any drink that looks like a blended Smurf and has the phrase *Adios* in its name is not something you should be ordering—ever.

Go to Yosemite with your father and bring plenty of beer. Get him drunk enough; you'll learn who the boy was that became this man you now struggle to know.

Finally—there's no easy way to say this, but she's cheating on you. A lot. Mourn if you must, but avoid sinking under the mass of an anvil heart. Carry your pain like a new tattoo that reads *survival* and ease into the rest of your days.

Feel weightlessness for the first time.

HOW TO LIE ON A BED OF NAILS
(for E.C.)

What we are practicing is suffering,
which everybody practices, but
strangely few of us grow graceful in.
                        —Tony Hoagland

It looks impossible—flesh pressed
against a thousand reasons to hurt.
Don't fool yourself into thinking this.
It is not magic, just pressure

divided across a body. Go slow.
Ease onto the bed with purpose.
Know what it is you suffer for, then
ask your nerve endings to stretch

over rows of tiny sharp reminders.
You may fear they will sink inches
deep, but the surface tension of each
being so close together will keep skin

from breaking. But to grow graceful
at it, you must practice. Rehearse.
Let it become dance, a soft waltz.
Trace a hand over the nails, feel

each slight scrape tingle your palm,
like static. Imagine this electricity
is not from waiting metal teeth, but
from taut dress fabric hugging the

small of a lover's back you have yet
to meet. Convince yourself of this,
until you forget the teeth altogether
so when you must finally perform

for a crowd, all anxious and rowdy,
they will be hushed, awestricken
by your daring act—by just how
effortless you make suffering appear.

IN CASE OF EMERGENCY, BREAK RIBS

You wear a wishbone around your neck,
hanging from a chain made of hope
like some dangle faith over their chest,
while others, diamonds that gleam

more than their own eyes. You tell me
it's in case you happen across emergencies
like me who have given up on wishing
three hearts ago. This one, my fourth, rests

behind a cage of ribs reinforced with iron,
barbed wire, and gun turret towers. I try
as hard to keep it from escaping as I do
others from entering. As far as wishes go,

I'm one of those who know shooting stars
are really just rock—falling space junk,
incinerating into glowing ghosts on their
way down. They are the ledge jumpers

of the universe. There's nothing wishful
about that. But you try to convince me
chaos like that is gorgeous—that a fall
like theirs can inspire so many to dream.

Explaining this, your lips become two
ready trapeze rings, waiting for my leap.
We kiss and each one of my ribs cracks,
breaking apart as if pulled by hands, each

eager to claim the larger piece of bone.
Exposed, my heart, that fist-shaped mass
of wishes, takes the plunge and together
we gaze at its brilliant tumbling descent.

WORKING THE ANGLES

Would you like to buy some chocolate for Jesus?
he asks, waving candy bars like tickets he's scalping
for a concert—one he's certain I want into.

It is September 2002. The sun is a violent lover—
I am more sweat than blood, and wonder what miracle
keeps chocolate from melting in his hands.

They're toffee, he points out,
as if it makes a difference.
I tell him, *No thanks.*

His smile is an accordion, stretching as he says,
Jesus loves you,
then compressing when I walk away.

The next day he's at it again, working the angles—
the overweight and under-will-powered,

old ladies with costume jewelry crosses
hanging from their necks like bullseyes,

parents of sugar-starved children who recognize
the word *no* as a grenade pin they don't dare pull.

He asks for charity from all but one—
a dark-skinned man in a turban.

Would it really offend Jesus
if offered chocolate from a Muslim?
Would the nougat be any less sweet?

He seems to think so,
and I am sad for this world.

Give me one instead where Jesus and Muhammad
sit around eating Hershey's Kisses,
waiting for Krishna to arrive with devil's food cake.

I AM A FORTUNE COOKIE

I'm always cracked open
for the clichés written inside me
with red ink.

All you want is petty reassurance
scribbled on paper
that true love is just around the corner.

You don't even eat me entirely.
I'm half the cookie I was
before you came along.

By the way
your true love has herpes.

Lucky Numbers: 3, 8, 12, 16, 21

WHERE LIGHT LIVES

It's no coincidence there are as many bars as churches here.
Both are easy places to fall into
when trying to be found—

when road maps show how to get lost,
and star maps point us out of LA,
towards the Midwest,
because the moon gets lonely here.

We all are lonely here, waiting
for angels on barstools and church pews
as if we're sitting in airport terminals
with our carry-on baggage in one hand
and *broken dreams* in the other,
sweating for our flights to take us
out of our skins and lift us into the sky.

But the stars that lit this runway once
left this place behind like an ex-lover,
and nothing has landed since.

Los Angeles is a shitty place to meet angels.

Live here long enough, you start to avoid this truth
as though it would turn you to ash—

convince yourself her wings must be caught
on some building's ledge like second thoughts
before a suicide, or with eyes so tear-drunk from smog,
she confuses sunsets for atom bombs
going off on the other side of the world.

Or maybe she's just stuck in traffic somewhere
moving slower than grief,
aching for a clean way out,
the open lane that will lead her straight to us.

Do not confuse this avoidance with hope.
That glowing torch does not come easy.

We're all looking for a little of it to call our own
that feels like a flare gun being fired in our chest,
but can't find a spark anywhere.
Most nights the soul is a dead language
buried inside us we will never understand,
and give up freely for just a little release.

But tonight let us struggle with it,
learn to read fire—the secret names
the constellations gave themselves
long before we ever called them stars.

We will see we are made of the same dust—
how all we ever needed was to find the light

in the hollow of our bones.

THOR LOSES HIS HAMMER

He staggers into my home tear-drunk,
gold locks reeking of booze and puke,
snot dangling from his perfect nose.
I ask, *What happened?*

It's gone, he says, *I can't find it.*

He sits, sinks into the cushions,
cries more than any god should.
Loki? I suggest, quick to help.

First place I tried—beat him to a pulp
then ransacked the underworld.
Hela told me to check with the frost giants.
No luck there, either.

As he speaks his voice shakes
with so much loss I ache for him—
helplessly, like having to see a child
break, bawling over a popped balloon.

I brew us coffee.
He takes his mug in his large god hands,
thanks me and asks what he should do.

Can't the dwarves just make another?

He says I don't understand.
Tells me it was a gift from Odin—
the only hard proof of his father's love.

But I do—years before my father left,
he gave me a watch I'd never wear,
but made promise to always keep.
Now it rests in a sleek black box,
tucked away in my bedside drawer.

Often I forget it is there, except
on nights I can't sleep, when I hear
its faint ticking, and think to take it
from its grave, to feel the weight
of my father's heart in my palm.

I want to tell Thor I understand,
but he has passed out on my couch,
curled into a muscular ball, snoring—
and I wonder,

if Thor cannot find his hammer,
how long before we all feel his loss,
how long before we miss the thunder
from our skies.

LITTLE DEATH

The first time your heart was torn from your chest,
you thought you were dying.

—Mindy Nettifee

When we first met, I knew you would be
the death of me, all curves and cast iron.

You were a sexy wrecking ball I could not
help but jump in front of. Your mouth was

a cyanide tablet and I wanted to swallow
your tongue. I could have slit my wrists

with your smiles—their corners' serrated
edges should come with better handling

instructions. And I admit I liked the way
you touched my neck maybe a little too

much. I could have fashioned nooses
from those fingers. You were so radical

I wanted to learn to speak terrorist and
take lessons in suicide bombing. You

were so intoxicating, alcohol poisoning
seemed like a good way to go—that is

to say I wanted to drink you all in so as
not to wake up the next morning beside

my regret. And that short black dress
you wore, the one that hugged your ass

like I wanted to—that might as well have
been my chalk outline, because you, naked,

were the ledge. The first time we made
love, I removed my parachute first—let it

hit the floor before I did. The first time we
made love, we did it in the lotus position,

used gasoline for lubricant, and lit a match.
My head spun faster than the bullet chamber

of a six-shooter loaded with five rounds.
I wished the gun had jammed that first time,

so things would have lasted a little longer
than they did, because that first time

we made love was our only time
and I've never felt more alive, dying.

ASPHYXIATE

Guiding my hand to your throat
as if it were nothing unusual
to ask of a new lover,
you whisper,
Choke me,
and I swear
if not for your eyes,
I would say no.
Cautious,
I shape my hand into an *L*
against the soft enclave
where neck meets clavicle,
thinking, *this should do.*
But you want more.
You wrap your fingers
over my own, showing
how tightly you need me
to hold you.
And like that first time
I slid my palm under a bra,
cupping flesh I had only
ever imagined,
I don't want to let go,
fearing I'll never find my way
back to this moment—so perfect,
so strange. You demand more
pressure. I feel powerful
and frightened all at once,
as the muscles of your throat
stiffen by reflex, jawbone
flush against the ridge
of my thumb and fingers,
my hand now closing
tighter and tighter around.
I squeeze and crush
and you come violently—
an animal thrashing about,
caught in steel teeth,
fighting to be free.

S&M

She wears similes like a leather bustier
accentuating all the right curves
and stands towering over me
on six-inch-high-heeled metaphors.

I turn submissive in her presence,
begging to be whipped by her words,
so they might leave letter-shaped welts
on my skin I can read with my fingers
all those times she blindfolds me.

I'd gladly give up control of my lungs
to her line breaks so they can be the force
commanding my breath, choking
me with their pauses just to make sure
I hang on her every thought.

I want to be tied down, restrained
by her sharp tongue while she cuts
into me with the English language,
so I can feel her hands go to work
inside my flesh transforming
me into a body of her writing.

She is poetry, a dominatrix,
and I am always her slave.

NIGHTMARE

I am naked—I am always naked
in these sorts of dreams.
All the girls I've ever slept with and
written poems about are in the audience,
whispering, giggling.

> *What the hell are they laughing at?*
> *This is a serious poem about father issues,*
> *the mortal coil, and unicycles.*
>
> *Oh yeah,*
> *I'm naked.*

Now there's no one in the crowd
but children. I am no longer nude—
thank God—but have twenty minutes
left to fill, and only four poems
not explicitly about, or referring to sex.

> *Fuck.*

I've already used up two of them.

> *Who the hell is this guy in the front*
> *talking on his cell phone, getting louder,*
> *as I try to read into the mic over him?*
> *Hey buddy, shut up!*

It's Jesus.
He's not too happy
with that one poem where I called Him
reduced-fat, making a bunch of weight jokes
at some poor parishioner's expense.

My thesis chair was right;
That poem was *too cruel.*
He holds up a score,
as if it were a slam.

5.9?
Come on Jesus,
That was at least an 8!

I am thirsty.
I garble my words.
My throat is wretched
with drought. I reach
for my whiskey. There's a straw
in it. I don't like straws in my whiskey.
I take it out, only to find another one
in its place. I toss it to the stage,
but yet another phantom straw appears.

> *Who the fuck keeps putting*
> *all these straws in my whiskey?*
> *Jesus, are you doing this?*

Just then a hermit crab
the size of a Volkswagen Bug scuttles
forward and tells me he's a prophet,
and to call him Frank.

"I am sorry to say, mon ami,"

—he has a French accent—

"but you will never again write another poem,
as good as your last one."

> *But my last poem was a haiku,*
> *nothing more than a dirty joke.*

"You should have thought of that before you wrote it."

He vanishes, and the spot on me fades.
Until the house goes dark
and I can no longer feel the stage
under my feet, until I am lost
in nothingness—and I'm falling.

I am falling.

DEAR READER, I DON'T TRUST YOU

If you were a sushi chef, I'd be suspect
of you serving me blowfish. If you tried
convincing me you were a respectable
dominatrix, I'd have trouble believing

you'd stop if I cried out the safe word.
And don't get me started on dark alleys.
For all I know, you're the creepy thing
lurking in shadows, all claws and fangs,

hungry to suck the life from my throat.
I wouldn't even trust you to have my
back in a bar fight. I've such a bad habit
for bluntness that you'd probably break

a bottle over my skull yourself if given
half the chance and an empty beer.
Sorry. It's nothing personal. As a writer,
I've been told I needed to earn your trust

before I should give you mine, but I'm
far too self-destructive for that. I'd rather
sabotage our relationship from the start
with a snarky title than put in all that work.

The effort it would take to get you to like
me could be better spent trying to write
the word *spine*, in fire, on my own back,
so I didn't need to rely on you to have mine.

Then, when I self-immolate into one burning
poem, sift though the ash and you'll find my
heart, shrunken, yet still intact—that perfect
metaphor you always wanted from me.

THE PROCEDURE

For fame and glory, you undergo the risk
of replacing your two lungs with blowtorches.

Many warn you'll never be the same after
the procedure. *Good*, you say, *That's the idea.*

Now a human dragon, you daydream of all
the thrilling jobs for credentialed fire breathers.

You update your resume, sprucing it up,
sure to mention how you can weld iron

with hands tied behind your back, control-burn
whole redwood forests with a puff, and star

in one-man pyrotechnic shows. But your talents
never find you any such line of work—nothing

as amazing as you first imagined for yourself,
back before your chest ever began to spark.

Rather, you're now reduced to a parlor trick,
going over well at cocktail parties, setting silly-

named drinks aflame, and you're a big hit
on camping trips, where you've mastered the art

of roasting marshmallows, crafting the perfect
s'more. When they cautioned, *you'll never*

be the same, this is not what you thought
they had meant—unsatisfied, unfulfilled

like some wretched matchstick in a wind tunnel,
or the thrusters of a rocket unable to combust

and take off from a world you believed
you were designed to escape.

ICARUS

Was Daedalus really stricken with grief when Icarus fell into the sea?
Or just disappointed by the design failure?

—*Alison Bechdel*

I.

My father once told me
he knew how to ride a unicycle.

I can't imagine him balancing
on one wheel—a clown
riding down the block
again and again, performing
for neighbors and friends
as they watched in awe
of his foolishness, waiting
to see if he'd lose it and fall.

I asked if he still knew how.

It's not like riding a bicycle,
he said.
You forget.

II.

Uncle Bill died, my father informs me
via text message.

I hardly remember my great uncle.

He hated the name William.
Wanted us to call him Bill
or Billy, said *William*
was his *father's* name.
It felt bitter
and metallic on his tongue—
a worn penny mistaken for candy.

I wonder if this is the same reason
my father, named for his *father*,
went by Dick rather than Richard.
The service is Friday morning
Can you make it? My father asks.
I'll try, I say.

III.

There are ghosts
haunting the silence
I've grown accustomed to
in our conversations. They linger
longer than usual before a heavy question.

So what are your plans after you finish school?

Poetry
isn't the response he wants—
it doesn't come with a business plan.
He sees it gaining little interest,
unable to cover the cost
of living, let alone dying.

You know,
if you die,
we'll be left
with your debt.

Words form angry mobs
in the back of my throat.
They want to storm the castle
walls my father's built between us.

I swallow them instead.
All I can say is *don't worry*.

IV.

He does worry.

I don't know if it's the money
or my *falling* which scares him more.

I like to think he's disappointed
in himself for forgetting, for becoming
the man he swore as a son he wouldn't—

wanting for me his own flawed designs,
sorry he did not name me after him.

CIRCUS LOVE

You're a big top circus—everything a boy dreams
of discovering under a red tent. The most dazzling woman

I've ever seen in a sequin leotard on top of an elephant.
You smell like peanuts, and I love peanuts, almost as much

as your sticky cotton candy kisses. When you perform
your acrobatic feats I want to enroll in contortionist school

just so I can learn to bend like you. You've got a flair
for the dangerous—you swallow swords, juggle knives,

and breathe fire all while riding a unicycle. Baby, you put the *pa*
in *panache*, so much so that those Ringling Brothers have

forfeited the title *greatest show on Earth* to you. If I could,
I'd be the trapeze you'd swing from, the tightrope you'd walk on,

and the safety net just in case you decided to fall for me.
What I wouldn't give to be the facial hair on your bearded lady,

your strongman's handlebar mustache, or your human
cannonball act. You make me want to wear over-sized shoes

and pants, change my name to Bozo and dance with a grizzly
bear in a tutu if it meant I had any chance of squeezing

into your clown car heart. But you are too savage a beast
for silliness like that—a wild lioness I'd never try to tame.

Instead, I'd gently request you open your mouth just wide
enough for me to rest my brow on your pink tongue,

where I would then wait patiently for your jaws to clamp shut,
so I could finally feel what it's like to lose my head.

TANDEM

I.

As a kid I was afraid to ride a bicycle,
puzzled by its strange mechanics, confused how one
stayed balanced on only two thin rubber wheels in motion.

I decided to leave it to the schoolyard daredevils.
Walking was fine for me.

But with the suckerpunch of puberty, my guts
were wound with enough messy bravery to finally learn how—
so I could slip out in the night with friends and TP the houses
of all the girls we liked.

We'd toss the rolls high over our heads like hand grenades,
spreading toilet paper as if it were the lining of our own hearts—
as if we were skywriting love notes against a canvas of midnight.

Rushing home after our confessions, we were champions
on ten speeds, free of words we had wanted to say,
but hadn't yet developed language for.

I was most alive, though, pedaling towards the girls,
appreciating how far I came to understand the balance
of it all, certain it was something I needed to know.

I could feel it in the way my muscles ached.

II.

On our first date, you tell me how solitude grew
to fit you well—how if a straitjacket is worn
long enough, it can become a favorite winter coat.

Two months later, you tell me a different story:
the beach, your sisters and their boyfriends,
two rented tandem bikes and a cruiser left for you
that was more torture device than bicycle.

It pulled a confession from your chest—
the word *lonely* escaped like a ghost
through the walls of your ribcage,
and has haunted you since.

Hearing this, I want to hold you with more arms
than I have—loot a prosthetic limbs factory
just to octopus-hug you when I whisper,

your beautiful autonomy makes single cell
organisms jealous, but eventually
even they learn to split in two.

What I don't say is this—

I hope your heart divides.
I hope I'm around to see its stunning symmetry,
maybe feel the weight of it rest in my palm
long enough to memorize its friction.

That kind of a confession, there's no language for.

So we sit silent. My eyes promising
I'll ride tandem bike marathons with you,
and yours answering back,

this is what we ached for.

ACKNOWLEDGMENTS

Grateful acknowledgement is made to the editors of the following publications in which these poems and stories have appeared, sometimes in varying form:

Beggars & Cheeseburgers: "Asphyxiate," "Racing Forward," "Repercussions"
Cobalt Poet Broadside Series: "Dear Reader, I Don't Trust You"
Connotation Press: "Little Death," "Nightmare"
Phantom Lips: "Things I'd Tell My 13-Year-Old Self (Had I a Time Machine)"
RipRap: "Lips"
San Pedro River Review: "Spackle"
Spot Lit: "Icarus," "The Procedure"
Verdad: "After this Morning," "Brass Knuckles," "Circus Love," "Open Heart Surgery," "S&M"

"I Am a Fortune Cookie" and "WWJD" appeared in *Carving in Bone: An Anthology of Orange County Poetry* (Moon Tide Press, 2007).

Thank you:

Moon Tide Press and Michael Miller, for publishing this, my very first, collection. Ricki Mandeville, for her admiration and keen editorial eye. Rob Sturma, for his gusto and inspiration—let us always storm Doom's castle together. Luke Salazar, Jessica Patapoff and Ben Trigg, my unofficial editors, who have each helped to shape many of the poems in this book. Greg Tovar, for covering more shifts than I can count, so I could be out at poetry readings. Friends and family, for their encouragement and support—especially Eubani Correa, Ray Lacoste, G. Murray Thomas, Mindy Nettifee, Vinatero Wine Shop and Daniel Morago. And of course, Katie O'Shaughnessy, my rock—I was writing poems about you long before we ever met, and a few since.

OTHER BOOKS FROM MOON TIDE PRESS

Lost American Nights: Lyrics & Poems
Michael Ubaldini
March 2006

Tide Pools: An Anthology of Orange County Poetry
June 2006

Sleepyhead Assassins
Mindy Nettifee
September 2006

A Thin Strand of Lights
Ricki Mandeville
December 2006

Kindness from a Dark God
Ben Trigg
June 2007

Carving in Bone: An Anthology of Orange County Poetry
December 2007

A Wild Region
Kate Buckley
April 2008

In the Heaven of Never Before
Carine Topal
December 2008

Now and Then
Lee Mallory
December 2009

Pop Art: An Anthology of Southern California Poetry
May 2010

LaVergne, TN USA
23 September 2010
198176LV00004B/7/P